MW01611113

THE MISSING LINK
OF MEDITATION

BILL WINSTON

The Missing Link Of Meditation

ISBN 978-1-63541-005-1

CONTENTS

v

INTRODUCTION

One man of God said that "Meditation is a missing link in the Body of Christ today." And I agree. Apart from hearing God's Word preached and studying the Word, meditation is the most important ingredient for spiritual growth and "good success."

This is why God told Joshua in Joshua 1:8 KJ21, *"This Book of the Law shall not depart out of thy mouth, but thou shalt meditate therein day and night, that thou mayest observe to do according to all that is written therein. For then thou shalt make thy way prosperous, and then thou shalt have good success."*

You see, there is a wisdom and an understanding that comes through meditation that is beyond common and intellectual sense. It is mainly the method that God provides to renew our minds and impart to us ingenious waves of creativity and abilities, enabling us to walk in dominion here on the earth.

I learned about biblical meditation many years ago as a new believer. By applying it in my life, I have had "good success" beyond anything I've ever dreamed, not only in ministry but in my personal life. Meditation is a spiritual law, and it works every time.

By reading this book, you will learn the power and importance of meditation, and how to bring all the unseen promises of God into manifestation into your life. If you have not been seeing the results the Bible promises, I believe this book will supply the "missing link" of meditation that will make your every dream become a reality.

Enjoy!

CHAPTER 1

WHAT IS MEDITATION?

Ecclesiastes 10 says,

> ⁵ There is an evil *which* I have seen under the sun, as an error *which* proceedeth from the ruler:

> ⁶ folly is set in great dignity, and the rich sit in low place.

> ⁷ I have seen servants upon horses, and princes walking as servants upon the earth.

This scripture describes, unfortunately, many in the Body of Christ.

Instead of being the lender and never having to borrow, many believe they have to be in debt up to their eyeballs. (I know I used to believe this.) Instead of being "the head" and dictating the terms of their existence, the majority of Christians have been "the tail." And when you are the tail, you get wagged...that means situations and circumstances controlling you rather than you in control.

Many people have heard the Word of God, some by preaching, others by teaching. Yet, in general, most of these same people are still at the same place spiritually they were five, ten, twenty, or thirty years ago when they first were born again. What's the problem? In most cases, it's a failure to **meditate** the Word that they heard.

Noah Webster's 1828 Dictionary defines *meditation* as **"close or contin- ued thought; the turning or revolv- ing of a subject in the mind; serious**

contemplation." Another definition describes *meditation* as **"to resolve in the
mind, imagine, or premeditate."**

Biblical meditation is simply turning the Word of God over in your heart
until it produces revelation or spiritual
sight. Meditating God's Word builds
faith, which allows you to see with your
spiritual eyes in the realm of the spirit.
*"Now faith is the assurance (the confir-
mation, the title deed) of the things [we]
hope for, being the proof of things [we] do
not see and the conviction of their reality
[faith perceiving as real fact what is not
revealed to the senses]," * (Hebrews 11:1
AMPC). Meditation also builds inner
strength to believe and the ability to hold
on to what you believe.

Genesis 24, verse 63, says, *"And
Isaac went out to meditate in the field at
the eventide: and he lifted up his eyes,
and saw, and behold, the camels were
coming."*

Isaac's meditation was probably a custom handed down to him from his father, Abraham. Notice it says, *"He lifted up his eyes."* This is the same expression used by Jesus describing the unseen harvest in the gospel of John, chapter four. And the same words used to describe the actions of Abraham (Genesis 22:13) when he, by faith, saw the *"ram caught in the thicket."* And the same phrase used to describe what was shown to Jacob in a dream to empower him to eventually possess everything his deceiving father-in-law, Laban, had. (Genesis 31:9-10)

The phrase "lifting up one's eyes" is another way to say seeing with one's spiritual eyes, or seeing in the realm of the spirit, which comes through meditation.

Meditation feeds the imagination and is our part in allowing the Holy Spirit to paint a vivid picture of our success and the truth of God's Word on the canvas of our soul. You actually see and believe God's promises before they are manifested. This all works on the principle of **seedtime and harvest**. When you meditate the Word of God, you are actually sowing good seed into your mind which will grow.

Meditation is what enabled Joshua and the nation of Israel to take possession of their inheritance, the Promised Land that, by the way, was full of giants. He commanded them in Joshua 1:8 to meditate on His Word while they worked during the day and during the quiet hours of the night. The *New Living Translation* says it this way, *"Study this Book of Instruction continually. Meditate on it day and night so you will be sure to obey everything written in it. Only then will you prosper and succeed in all you do."*

CHAPTER 2

YOU CAN CHANGE YOUR MIND

Meditation is a God-given process that causes a permanent change in your thinking. In other words, meditation transforms your thinking from ungodly thoughts and lies programmed into the mind mainly by a demon-controlled world system, to conform to thinking God's thoughts...in an accelerated manner.

Remember when the twelve spies returned from spying out the Promised Land? Numbers 13:32 says, *"And they brought up an evil report."* Ten of the spies (leaders) reported something to the congregation that was not the Word or the will of God. The scriptures go on to say, *"And all the congregation lifted up their voices, and cried; and the people wept that night"* (Numbers 14:1). They meditated (pondered) and quickly began to visualize the worst, never even physically seeing one single giant.

Instead of this large congregation meditating on the two spies' "good report," the report of the Lord, they chose to meditate on the "evil report," the bad news. And just like a seed sown in soil, it came to harvest. They received exactly what they believed and spoke, dying without ever reaching their destiny. **I decree that you will have a long life and you will reach your God-given destiny, in Jesus' Name!**

THE POWER OF MEDITATION

Once you start meditating something out of the Word of God, it begins to affect your **imagination** and how you see things. You begin to see yourself and your situation the way God sees them. And here's an awesome truth. If you see it, believe it and act on it in faith, your success is GUARANTEED (Joshua 1:8 AMP).

Someone might ask, "How do I see something that is not there, that does not exist?" Here's the secret. <u>The will of God is already in existence, in the eternal, invisible realm.</u> But like the donkey Jesus rode into Jerusalem on, you have to call for it. God said to Abraham, *"...Lift up now thine eyes...For all the land which thou seest, to thee will I give it, and to thy seed forever,"* (Genesis 13:14-15).

Again, God spoke to Joshua as he was about to possess Jericho, a city that was "naturally" impossible to penetrate, *"See, I have given into thy hands Jericho, and the king thereof, and the mighty men of valor"* (Joshua 6:2).

With God, you have TO SEE it before He can deliver it or before you can physically have it manifested. A blind man can't go where he can't see; it is nearly impossible. Satan could see the hedge protecting Job, but Job couldn't see it (Job 1:10), resulting in satan robbing Job of everything he had.

In the New Testament, there was a man named Bartimaeus who was physically blind and sat by the highway side begging. He heard Jesus was passing by and began to cry out—He was physically blind but had a revelation of Jesus as the Healer and Miracle Worker. Bartimaeus SAW his healing, and it was delivered to him at that moment. He was miraculously healed.

In the book of Acts, chapter 10 (KJ21), God used a vision to transform the apostle Peter's thinking, which helped revolutionize the New Testament Church. Peter went up to pray on the house top just before his noon meal, and as he prayed, he fell into a trance. (Sometimes, meditation works better on an empty stomach, or early in the morning or late at night when it is quiet.) Here's what the scriptures say,

⁹ On the morrow, as they went on their journey and drew nigh unto the city, Peter went up upon the house-top to pray about the sixth hour.

¹⁰ And he became very hungry and would have eaten; but while they were making ready he fell into a trance,

¹¹ and saw heaven opened and a certain vessel descending unto him as though it had been a great sheet knit at the four corners and let down to the earth,

¹² wherein were all kinds of four-footed beasts of the earth, and wild beasts and creeping things and fowls of the air.

¹³ And there came a voice to him, "Rise, Peter; kill and eat."

¹⁴ But Peter said, "Not so, Lord, for I have never eaten anything that is common or unclean."

¹⁵ And the voice spoke unto him again the second time, "What God hath cleansed, that call not thou common."

This vision prepared Peter to go to Cornelius, a centurion who was a devout man and feared God but was not a Jew. This was a significant break with Jewish tradition.

²⁸ And he (Peter) said unto them, "Ye know that it is an unlawful thing for a man who is a Jew to keep company with or to come unto one of another nation. But God hath shown me that I should not call any man common or unclean.

Through the vision, Peter had this revelation, *"In truth I perceive that God is no respecter of persons, but in every nation he that feareth Him and worketh righteousness is accepted by Him,"* (verses 34-35 KJ21). I have quoted this scripture many times on the mission field. I have to let the audiences know that God is not blessing because of a certain person's color or country. God blesses you because you are a believer.

Meditation brings a **Revelation** (spiritual sight) that causes a **Revolution.** You can actually believe or imagine to the point where you develop what I call…"Crazy Faith." This happens when what you see in your mind becomes more real than your circumstances outside around you. "Crazy faith" is a level of faith where our minds are no longer governed by what makes sense.

CHAPTER 3

MEDITATION CREATES A NEW REALITY

Some years ago, as we ended our last Sunday service, God spoke to my heart and said, "Buy that mall." (Across the street from where we held our worship services was an empty shopping mall.) This was something that seemed impossible for a number of reasons, among them, our church didn't have that kind of money, and I didn't know anything about the shopping mall business.

Well, God fixed all of that by having me **meditate.** He gave me the seed (Word) which came from Joshua 1:3 and I meditated it day and night, *"Every place that the sole of your foot shall tread* *upon, that have I given unto you....*" I soon "saw" it clearer than with my natural eyes...and what I saw is what God delivered.

Daily, we are surrounded by hostile forces in a hostile world that oppose God, where most people are going through life based on a prior mental program derived from ignorance, unbelief and "fake news."

Meditation causes a "rewrite" and destruction of the old, negative Babylonian, fallen-man thinking and replaces it with the thoughts and plans God has for us, His children. *"For I know the plans and thoughts that I have for you,' says the Lord, 'plans for peace and well-being and not for disaster to give you a future and a hope"* (Jeremiah 29:11 AMP)

DESTROYING UNGODLY IMAGES

In 1 Kings 18:21, the prophet Elijah was confronting the prophets of Baal (a very common name for god among the heathen nations). He challenged them to call on the name of their god to send fire to consume the sacrifice—and they could not. He proceeded to prepare the altar and called on the one true God.

The fire fell from heaven and miraculously burned up the sacrifice and everything. The prophets of Baal then cried, *"The Lord, He is God! The Lord, He is God!"* (verse 39). Many times when the Lord does a miracle in your life, it destroys the old image that trusting in the world and its system has produced.

In Mark, chapter five, there was a woman who had an issue of blood for twelve years. The scripture says, *"She had gone to many physicians and was nothing bettered, but rather grew worse. When she had heard of Jesus, came in the press and touched his garment. For she said, if I may touch his clothes, I shall be whole. And straightway the fountain of her blood was dried up; and she felt in her body that she was healed of that plague."* The *Amplified Bible* says she had heard the reports concerning Jesus and she kept saying (verses 27, 28). To meditate is to speak to yourself, repeatedly... not the problem but the answer.

Here's the point. <u>You cannot enjoy the "Promises" and the "Plenty" of God without first destroying the ungodly images that have been sown (built) into your subconscious</u>. The subconscious mind is designed to keep us in line with what we believe, even if it's a lie. What's outside of you is a product of what's inside of you. (Matthew 12:34-35)

An inner image of lack will never produce an outer manifestation of plenty or abundance. An inner image of sickness will never produce an outward manifestation of healing and wholeness. Hear the woman's continuous confession of her future, *"if I may touch his clothes, I shall be whole."* She was destroying the "grow worse" image that was built inside her through constantly hearing and meditating an evil report that she was getting worse, and was creating **a new reality**.

MY STORY: LEAVING IBM

I used the power of meditation when God was telling me to leave my (very good) job at IBM and go into full-time ministry. I knew God had called me into full-time ministry, but I did not have the strength to step out and leave my good-paying job at IBM. Oh, I had tried several times, but until I could SEE my future, I was stuck in my present. Then, I heard a man of God teach on seedtime and harvest. Out of that, God gave me a seed (scripture), Mark 10:29-30.

[29] And Jesus answered and said, Verily I say unto you, There is no man that hath left house, or brethren, or sisters, or father, or mother,

or wife, or children, or lands, for my
sake, and the gospel's,

[30] but he shall receive an hundred-
fold now in this time, houses, and
brethren, and sisters, and mothers,
and children, and lands, with per-
secutions; and in the world to come
eternal life.

I began meditating what God gave me
and in a very short time, POW! Light
came! I saw myself preaching the gospel
to 10,000 people...NOT GOING BROKE. I
saw myself leaving corporate and serving
God full-time in a successful ministry.
I saw a GLORIOUS FUTURE, and now
I could let go of the "job" I was holding
on to.

I went to my boss and told him, "I'm
leaving the company." (Now, the company
had been good to me and had big plans
for me, but it was time to obey God.) He

jumped up and closed the door behind us. I explained to him that I was following my calling and that I had to leave. He immediately said, "Bill, take two weeks off." He thought I had been working too hard and needed a vacation. Be aware; people might think that about you when you see something that they can't see.

Just like the vision of the apostle Peter, as I meditated Mark 10:29-30, the Holy Spirit brought a **Revelation** which caused a **Revolution** in my life. And <u>what I saw is what God delivered.</u> Today, our ministry is preaching the gospel to hundreds of millions of households weekly around the world through television and other media. And we have offices in Canada, South Africa, and soon, Australia.

Remember, what we can't see, we cannot become. This is why meditation is so important. Meditation is the way to secure your future without struggle.

Chapter 4

Meditation:
A Spiritual law

As mentioned earlier, when God turned over the leadership of the children of Israel to Joshua, Moses' protégé, God instructed Joshua on the key ingredient for his success:

> This book of the law shall not depart out of thy mouth; but thou shalt meditate therein day and night, that thou mayest observe to do according to all that is written therein: for then thou shalt make thy way prosperous, and then thou shalt have good success (Joshua 1:8).

Meditation of God's Word (biblical meditation) was the key ingredient, and it was something they were commanded. It was not an option. God commanded His people to meditate His Word throughout history because it is spiritual law and how the kingdom of God operates in the earth. Here are some examples:

Abraham meditated on the stars that God showed him when He said, *"...Look now toward heaven, and tell the stars, if thou be able to number them: and He said unto him, So shall thy seed be"* (Genesis 15:5).

Isaac went out to meditate just before dusk. This was probably a custom that was handed down to him from his father, Abraham. *"And Isaac went out to meditate in the field at eventide ..."* (Genesis 24:63).

King David meditated God's Word. In the book of Psalms, David writes, *"I call to remembrance my song in the night: I commune* (meditate) *with mine own heart: and my spirit made diligent search"* (Psalm 77:6). *"Mine eyes prevent the night watches, that I might meditate in thy word"* (Psalm 119:148).

For David, meditation was a time of fellowship with the Lord, a time of worship and praise, which draws the presence of God. When we meditate, our spirit makes "diligent search." This is our heart (spirit) reaching for guidance, answers or making new discoveries in God's Word.

David said, *"I will meditate on all thy work, and muse on thy mighty deeds"* (Psalm 77:12 RSV). To *muse* means to "ponder, meditate, or reflect." Whenever the scriptures read, "I will," it means that you have a decision to make. The choice is yours. The Scriptures counsel us to always choose the Word of God and believe only what it says.

Biblical meditation is designed to renew your mind and expand your capacity to receive the promises of God in your life. It is a way to transform your thinking, so you can think on a higher level—on the frequency of God. Remember, if something is too big for your mind, it will be too big for your hand.

Conclusion

Psalm 1 says,

> [1] Blessed *is* the man that walketh not in the counsel of the ungodly, nor standeth in the way of sinners, nor sitteth in the seat of the scornful.

> [2] But his delight *is* in the law of the Lord; and in his law doth he MEDITATE day and night.

> [3] And he shall be like a tree planted by the rivers of water, that bringeth forth his fruit in his season; his leaf also shall not wither; and whatsoever he doeth shall prosper.

God wants our thoughts to be in agreement with His thoughts, which are in His Word. When you meditate, you are actually sowing "Word seed" into your mind which will grow. Whatever you sow, you will eventually see manifest in your life, good or bad, true or not true. What you believe will always become your reality. Proverbs 23:7 says, *"For as he thinketh in his heart, so is he...."*

In closing, here are four keys to successful biblical meditation:

1) Meditation – Meditate on a success truth or "seed" that corresponds with the thing or promise you desire from God's Word. The Holy Spirit will help you.

2) Visualization – Imagine (ponder, muse, speak over and over) until you see it happening to you, like being a top salesperson or having a happy marriage.

3) Actualization – Act on what you see when it becomes revelation.

4) Manifestation – Experience the physical reproduction of what you have already experienced on the inside.

If you have not been meditating, try starting with the next assignment given to you by God, or with the next problem caused by the adversary. Allow the Holy Spirit to direct your thoughts and reveal to you what scripture (seed) to use to think on.

Meditate this Word until you transform your belief—until you see the future on the canvas of your soul. The act releases your faith to manifest what God has planned and what Jesus died to provide. Remember, there is nothing He can give that He has not already given. Selah!

WILLIAM (BILL) SAMUEL WINSTON

Bill Winston is the visionary founder and senior pastor of **Living Word Christian Center**, a 20,000-member church with headquarters in Forest Park, Illinois.

He is also founder and president of **Bill Winston Ministries**, a partnership-based global outreach ministry that shares the gospel through television, radio, and the internet; the nationally accredited **Joseph Business School** which has partnership locations on five continents and an online program; the **Living Word School of Ministry and Missions**; and **Faith Ministries Alliance (FMA)**, an organization of over 800 churches and ministries under his spiritual covering in the United States and other countries.

The ministry owns and operates two shopping malls, **Forest Park Plaza** in Forest Park and **Washington Plaza** in Tuskegee, Alabama. Bill Winston is also the founder and CEO of **Golden Eagle Aviation**, a fixed base operator (FBO) located at the historic Moton Field in Tuskegee.

Bill is married to Veronica and is the father of three, Melody, Allegra, and David, and the grandfather of eight.

BOOKS BY BILL WINSTON

- Born Again and Spirit Filled (Available in English, Polish and Spanish versions)
- Climbing Without Compromise
- Divine Favor – A Gift from God, Expanded Edition
- Faith & The Marketplace
- Imitate God and Get Results (Available in English and French versions)
- Possessing Your Mountain
- Power of the Tongue
- Seeding For the Billion Flow
- Supernatural Wealth Transfer: Restoring the Earth to Its Rightful Owners
- Tapping the Wisdom of God
- The God Kind of Faith

- The Kingdom of God In You: Discover the Greatness of God's Power Within
- The Law of Confession: Revolutionize Your Life and Rewrite Your Future with the Power of Words
- The Power of Grace
- The Power of the Tithe
- Training For Reigning: Releasing the Power of Your Potential
- Transform Your Thinking, Transform Your Life: Radically Change Your Thoughts, Your World, and Your Destiny

Connect With Us!

Connect with Bill Winston Ministries on Social Media. Visit <u>www.billwinston.org/social</u> to connect with all of our official Social Media channels.

Bill Winston Ministries

P.O. Box 947
Oak Park, Illinois 60303-0947
(708) 697-5100
(800) 711-9327
www.billwinston.org

Bill Winston Ministries Africa

22 Salisbury Road
Morningside, Durban, KWA Zulu
Natal 4001
+27(0)313032541 orders@bwm.org.za
<u>www.bwm.org.za</u>

Bill Winston Ministries Canada

P.O. Box 2900
Vancouver BC V6B 0L4
(844) 298-2900

Prayer Call Center

(877) 543-9443